THE FUTURE OF AMERICAN PROGRESSIVISM

ROBERTO MANGABEIRA

UNGER

&

CORNEL

WEST

THE FUTURE OF AMERICAN
PROGRESSIVISM

AN INITIATIVE FOR POLITICAL AND ECONOMIC REFORM

BEACON PRESS BOSTON

Beacon Press
25 Beacon Street
Boston, Massachusetts 02108-2892
www.beacon.org

Beacon Press books
are published under the auspices of
the Unitarian Universalist Association of Congregations.

03 02 01 00 99 98   8 7 6 5 4 3 2 1

This book is printed on recycled acid-free paper that contains at least 20 percent
postconsumer waste and meets the uncoated paper ANSI/NISO specifications for
permanence as revised in 1992.

Text design by Elizabeth Elsas

Library of Congress Cataloging-in-Publication Data

Unger, Roberto Mangabeira.
The future of American progressivism : an initiative for political and economic
reform / Roberto Mangabeira Unger and Cornel West.
    p.   cm.
ISBN 0-8070-4326-5 (hardcover : alk. paper)
1. United States—Politics and government—1993– 2. United States—Economic
policy—1993– 3. Progressivism (United States politics)   I. West, Cornel.   II. Title.
JK271.U533 1998
320.973—dc21

                                                              98-26791

CONTENTS

CHAPTER 1
THE HUMANIZATION OF THE INEVITABLE

Open almost any mainstream newspaper or news magazine in the world today, and you will find the news of the world shaped by the same story line. The line goes like this. After the collapse of communism, thinking people all over the planet finally came to agree that there is only one reliable road to freedom and prosperity. To enter this road, every country must establish some version of the political and economic institutions that have long been secure in the United States and much of Western Europe. The move often requires painful adjustment, austerity, and sacrifice. There are many obstacles and surprises along the way. However, the direction of the path is not in doubt.

The social misery that may come, initially, with conformity to the path triggers a populist backlash. People rebel against the increasing inequality, joblessness, or insecurity that taking the one true way sometimes causes. The rebellion is likely to be most vigorous in the societies that must travel furthest to reach the fork toward the right road: the developing countries of Latin America and Africa or the postcommunist countries of Eastern Europe and Asia. There, a ragtag assortment of neocommunists, nationalists, and demagogues try, usually without much success, to ride the wave of popular resentment. Even Western Europe, with its entrenched social-democratic traditions, needs adjustments. Inefficient industries, high unemployment, and unsustainable deficits make European leaders of the center-left as well as the center-right anxious to reconcile European-style social protections with American-style market flexibility.

Their efforts speak to a universal concern. The doctrine of the one true way claims to describe the inevitable in politics and economics. Insofar as possible, however, the inevitable, according to those who tell this story, should be humanized: the arrangements implementing the inevitable should compensate for individual hardship. By combining adjustments to the free market with programs to help the poor and the jobless, without destroying their incentive to work, we ensure decency and prevent the populist backlash from getting out of hand. Thus, the humanization of the inevitable, the attempt to make the one true way less cruel to those who suffer on the road to freedom and prosperity, becomes the watchword of chastened progressives everywhere. Their program becomes the program of their adversaries—with a discount, and a falling one at that.

There is, however, at least one country in the world where the doctrine of the one true way and its companion, the humanization of the inevitable, remain insecure. That country is the winner of the Cold War; it enjoys unrivaled cultural, political, and economic leadership in the world; and is supposedly the very embodiment of the one true way. That country is the United States.

The oldest and most American element of American life is the religion of individual and collective possibility: the belief that Americans can make themselves and remake their society, that they can make everything new. The American dream includes a middle-class standard of living for everyone, with economic independence and security, as well as opportunites for people's children to achieve what their parents failed to accomplish or obtain. It also relies upon a more intangible but immensely powerful idea of freedom from being bossed around in one's choice of life, tastes, and beliefs.

Today, however, at the apogee of its world power and in the midst of an economy thriving as rarely before, most working Americans feel more squeezed than ever, and convinced that life will be harder for them than it was for their parents. Even politically active and educated elites feel incapable of addressing, much less solving, many of the basic problems of the country, from inadequate health care and education to the social and racial apartheid of inner-city poverty, from increasing inequality of wealth and income to abstention from the vote and indifference to politics. The practical consequence of this national failure is that Americans despair of collective solutions to their collective problems, and alternate between resenting the incapable politics of their country and blaming themselves for failure to succeed at a game that so often seems rigged against them.

The young in the elite universities—the youth of an imperial power—feel the more disenchanted the more serious they are, as if they had been born at the wrong place and the wrong time, as if everything interesting in the world were happening somewhere else. The size of the country, and the decentralization of power and influence within it, play a part in their frustration: almost any measure of influence an individual can hope to gain seems dwarfed by the sheer bigness and variety of the United States. So does the absence from national life of anything other than a politics of inconclusive bargaining among organized interests about minor fix-its. In this American circumstance the triumphalism of the doctrine of the one true way rings hollow. National triumph goes hand in hand with individual impotence.

CHAPTER 2
THE AMERICAN RELIGION OF POSSIBILITY

Speaking in Madison Square Garden during his unsuc-
cessful campaign for reelection as president of the
United States, Herbert Hoover summarized the quin-
tessential American self-conception when he said: "It is
by the maintenance of equality of opportunity and
therefore of a society absolutely fluid in freedom of the
movement of its human particles that our individualism
departs from the individualism of Europe. We resent
class distinction because there can be no rise for the individual through the frozen strata of classes and no

stratification of class can take place in a mass livened by the free rise of its particles." Not even the people standing in bread lines outside could impress upon Hoover the incongruity of seeing the country as a collection of free-floating particles rising and falling in an unresisting social medium.

Hoover was describing a facet of the American religion of possibility. In America, men and women have placed hope above memory. They have believed that the future remains open to national renewal as well as to individual self-transformation. They have refused to believe that anything in their situation condemns them to languish in permanent poverty, dependency, and weakness. They have rejected the idea that their country was locked by its history into an orbit of familiar solutions to recurrent problems. They have insisted that, both as individuals and together, people can confront and defeat the forces that prevent them from living more fully and freely.

Hoover's claims highlight the social side of this idea of possibility. It is the belief that everyone can lift themselves up from the bottom, and win power to shape their immediate circumstances. In their own lifetime and the lifetimes of their children, they can escape penury and subjection, and achieve a measure of independence. A family farm, a small independent business, or a stable, respectable job in an organization or profession, have been the most traditional bases of such an independence. According to this idea of social opportunity, class distinctions in America have never become so rigid as to prevent the rise of the individual.

Individual effort remains the primary instrument of self-empowerment. There may often be obstacles to this free movement of the "human particles" that individual self-reliance is unable, unassisted, to overcome. Collective action may then become necessary: people working together in their communities, jobs, churches, and clubs. To be effective, according to the dominant version of the American religion of possibility, such a joint effort must be uncoerced. Above all, it must never be commandeered and orchestrated by government except in extreme situations or over a narrow, well-defined range of problems.

According to this view, voluntary association does not suffice to make self-reliance effective for the broad masses of ordinary Americans. Governmental action may also be needed to make self-reliance work. There are many basic needs—like the requirement of universal public education—that will always demand initiative by government. Sometimes a great crisis, or the accumulated effect of slow but profound changes in the organization of the society and the economy, may require an expansion of governmental activism. In its form and scope, however, such an expansion should be careful to respect the primacy of individual initiative and free association.

There has almost always been just enough opportunity in America to make this facet of the American religion of possibility plausible. Each epoch in American history witnesses its own paradoxical developments, extending social mobility in some respects while limiting it in others. Today, for example, there is evidence that, while the differences between rich and poor have widened, the role of inherited advantage, the hereditary transmission of property and inherited educational opportunity, has diminished.

The admissions practices of universities and the hiring practices of professional firms and big business have slowly extended the reign of meritocracy. The meritocratic opening may be less significant for members of the working class, with the notable exception of the strengthening of restraints on discrimination against people defined by the physically inscribed characteristics of race, gender, or handicap. However, working-class men and women may find it harder than ever to grasp the structure of privilege and inequality in the country. The institutional complexity and regional variety of this structure, its wealth of manifestations and qualifications, keep it from being readily visible.

Faith in the power of the individual to better his or her life is the most prominent element in the American religion of possibility, but it is not the only or even the most important one. That religion also includes something more basic and something more ambitious: a belief in the unlimited potential of practical problem solving and a faith in democracy as a terrain on which ordinary men and women can become strongly defined personalities, in full possession of themselves.

The United States is a country of tinkerers. To hold the American religion of possibility is to believe that each of the problems that oppress, weaken, and frighten us as individuals can be confronted, problem by problem, through human effort and ingenuity. Americans resist seeing particular problems as the manifestation of hidden, hard constraints. They believe that the terrors of vast problems yield to the effects of many small solutions.

Use little things to break big things, says Saint Paul, describing an essential feature of the psychology of hope.

For hope is more the consequence of action than its cause. As the experience of the spectator favors fatalism, so the experience of the agent produces hope. A preference for acting over watching has been the most important consequence of the problem-solving attitude.

Social opportunity as a condition and problem solving as an attitude fail to describe the most potent and fundamental strand in the American religion of possibility: *faith in the genius of ordinary men and women*. Walt Whitman, in the secular bible of democracy, *Democratic Vistas*, cited John Stuart Mill's discussion of the twin attributes of a great nation living under liberty, redescribing them as central ambitions of American democracy: first, a large variety of character and second, full play for human nature to expand itself in numberless and even conflicting directions. The capacity for strong and original experience, rather than being confined to a small number of geniuses, heroes, and eccentrics, should become widespread among ordinary people.

This belief in the elevation of ordinary humanity contrasts with the pressures to conformity that have played so powerful a role in American life. Intolerance of actual difference—difference of experience and vision—flourished amid the celebration of outward group distinctions. Yet the idea persists that no closed elite enjoys a privileged hold upon the capacity for extraordinary effort, experience, and achievement.

The soul of the ordinary man and woman hides vast recesses of intensity. The sadness of much human life lies in the disproportion between this intensity and the accidental or unworthy objects on which people so often lavish their intense commitments. That this reserve capacity for devotion and obsession can be tapped productively, for the good of the community as well as the individual, has always been a major tenet of the American religion of possibility. Democracy, Americans understand, depends upon *demophilia*, love of the people.

Here we encounter another subtle and paradoxical element of the American faith in the possible. A distrust of collective enthusiasms, especially when they seek to work through the power of government, has always been an integral part of the American faith. Thus, that faith contains a basis for the "countermajoritarian restraints" so famously prized by American constitutional tradition.

Trouble for American democracy and for the American imagination of the possible arises when disappointment with the results of popular democracy leads to a perversion to which American democracy has often been subject: the effort to use the countermajoritarian power of a judicial elite to impose through judicial lawmaking what the people through their elected representatives are unwilling to achieve themselves.

There then begins a self-reinforcing cycle of popular political disempowerment. The oppressed minorities or social victims are defined as the wards of a cadre of enlightened and benevolent notables. As politics shrinks in scope and wanes in practical effect, the people lose interest in it and seek to cut their losses. They resist, for example, the substantial tax take required to fund the programs of an activist government. The political incapacity of the people becomes a self-confirming prophecy. What starts as a way to protect the many-sidedness of the future against the single-mindedness of the present ends as an outright expression of *demophobia*, fear of the people.

We shall later ask whether the present constitutional arrangements of the country strike the right balance between demophilic hopes and demophobic anxieties, and strike it in the way most faithful to the American religion of possibility.

CHAPTER 3
THE BURDEN OF AMERICAN HISTORY ON AMERICAN HOPES

The religion of individual and collective possibility in the United States has always suffered under three great burdens: the enduring power of hierarchies of class, race, and gender as well as the inhibiting effect of their entanglement in each other; the sometimes narrow-minded obsession with individual self-reliance and self-improvement that obscures the dependence of individual life chances upon collective arrangements; and the failure to submit the country's basic institutions to the experimentalist impulse that is otherwise so strong in America.

When asked to what social class they belong, Americans in overwhelming numbers answer that they belong to the middle class. The truth, however, is that the United States has a relatively well-defined class structure, if by class structure we mean the division of people into large social groups, shaped by the twin forces of property and educational advantage transmitted through families. There are four main social classes in the United States: a class of high-power professionals and big-business executives, a small-business class, a working class (with both a blue-collar and a white-collar segment), and a racially stigmatized underclass. Each of these classes is marked by distinctive experiences of power and powerlessness at work, characteristic lifestyles and self-images, and access to different types of jobs and to the levels of wealth and income that go along with them.

In American history, the greatest experience of social mobility has been the frequency with which the children of farmhands and industrial workers became white-collar workers, moving from the blue-collar to the white-collar segment of the working class. Recent studies suggest that in the last fifteen years the influence of inherited advantage upon individual life chances has diminished (thanks in part to the more meritocratic selection procedures of universities, big business, and the professions), while economic inequality has increased. A large part of the population remains below the economic and educational threshold it must pass to profit from merit-based selection procedures. It is a benefit to Americans that, like Herbert Hoover, they deny legitimacy to class. It is a detriment that, also like him, they have usually been unwilling or unable to recognize its force in their national life. *The basic design of the class system has remained as stable in American reality as it has been clouded in American consciousness.*

The most important complication of the American class system is the unique way in which it has combined with racial oppression and prejudice. Race has always been America's rawest nerve and most explosive issue— as manifest in our Civil War and uncivil urban uprisings. Indigenous peoples, Latinos, and Asians have been integral to the making of the country from the begining, yet the presence of black people often overshadows this truth. The legacy of white supremacy affects them all despite the centrality of black subordination in American discourses of race.

The common problems of white, black, brown, red, and yellow working people came to be hidden by the racial divisions that set them apart. Needless to say, the vicious legacies of male supremacy and homophobia continue to plague us. The historical weight of class and race appears indirectly in stubborn divisions and many-sided inhibitions. The progressive forces in the country have been faced at every turn with a paralyzing dilemma in which they remain caught to this day. If they seek to redress racial injustice before class injustice, they risk helping the elites of the oppressed races while leaving the rank and file sunk in poverty, ignorance, and exclusion. At the same time, they excite resentments that prevent the formation of a progressive majority of working-class people of all races. If, on the other hand, they insist upon dealing with racial and class injustices simultaneously, they risk sacrificing the feasible good to the unreachable best: support for this more ambitious program may fail to build while racial oppression may go unchallenged.

Black slavery, in particular, inflicted upon American democracy a wound from which it has never fully recovered. Two things have always seemed impossible in America. One is to keep the descendants of the African slaves chained and resigned to their chains; the other is to treat them as equals to white Americans. Even today, under the disguise of thick political pieties, blacks remain the "problem people" of which Du Bois spoke, their very existence in the United States a rebuke and a threat. With the failure of the early attempt during Reconstruction to liberate the freed slaves from the economic and educational consequences of their enslavement, blacks were abandoned to a subjugation from which half of them have only recently emerged.

If the first constraint upon the American religion of possibility has been the poisonous mixture of race and class, the second has been a narrow-minded conception of self-reliance and self-improvement as the popular public morality of the country. Americans have wanted and claimed to be men and women who invent and crown themselves. Some of their most characteristic thinkers—from Ralph Waldo Emerson to Ralph Waldo Ellison—have taught a doctrine of individual self-reliance pushed to the point of denying connection and vulnerability. Thinking of themselves as having made an all but definitive escape from the old European history of classes, privileges, and ideologies, Americans have often found it hard to combine an ethic of personal striving with practical insight into the collective and institutional limits to their efforts at lifting themselves up, individual by individual and family by family. In the absence of such insight they have regularly oscillated between blaming themselves for all their problems and attributing them to the malevolent conspiracies of the people who run the show in politics and business.

The denial of need—of the raw neediness of every human being—and the obsession with control—control of whatever makes us vulnerable to others—have inspired endless practices of physical and pyschological self-improvement, from bodybuilding to popular Freudianism, while sustaining a low-level hysteria about elementary human drives and weaknesses, as witnessed in our national obsession with sexual scandal. No wonder that in the United States, violence, the rage of control, has often seemed more acceptable than sex, a door to vulnerability. No wonder the unequaled private generosity of Americans, expressed in a willingness to give time as well as money to those in need, has coexisted with an unwillingness to acknowledge public obligations of social solidarity.

The third taint upon the religion of possibility in the United States has been the reluctance of Americans to subject their basic institutional arrangements to the experimentalist impulse so vital in so many aspects of

American life. Faith in the capacity of ordinary people to solve practical problems has been one of the most striking characteristics of the country. The United States is rich and powerful because it is a country of experimenters. Motivated, sustained, and cumulative tinkering with institutional arrangements is an indispensable tool of democratic experimentalism, of improvisational reform, of jazzlike public action.

Americans, however, have been willing to use this tool only under the extreme pressure of crisis and catastrophe. There have been three great periods of institutional innovation in American history: the foundation of the Republic, the Civil War and Reconstruction, and the New Deal. In each, national leaders won support for institutional experiments from an energized majority. After the first of these three periods of collective creation, however, the country has been attracted to the idea that, at the time of its independence, it came close to the natural and necessary form of a free society.

According to this powerful strand in American ideas, the United States was different less because of its devotion to the religion of possibility than because it had early achieved a fix on the institutional form of a free society: Hoover's natural space of the rising and falling individuals. There were ordeals to undergo—the terrible burden of slavery and its aftermath, a massive economic failure, or the outbreak of war in Europe— and crisis might require adjustment. But such innovations as were needed to improve society would result mainly from the independent initiative of people in their businesses or the voluntary association of individuals in their communities. Exceptions like the G.I. Bill or Civil Rights Bill, triggered by grassroots groups like the American Legion or black churches, prove the rule.

A small number of major American thinkers, like Thomas Jefferson, Abraham Lincoln, Henry George, W. E. B. Du Bois, Ida B. Wells-Barnett, and John Dewey, tried to convince Americans to lift the exemption from experimentalism they accorded to their institutions, and to trade in some bad American exceptionalism for some good American experimentalism. Their message, however, was only selectively heard, even by the progressive movements in American history whose rigid, ideological grids often overlook the complexity and experimental impulse of American life.

If American progressivism is to be reborn today and to carry forward its work, if it is to keep the religion of possibility alive and loosen the constraints that racial and gender oppression and class hierarchy impose upon American democracy, if it is to go beyond the humanization of the inevitable to a better state of freedom and possibility, it must hear that message of democratic experimentalism more clearly. Progressives must present to the country a reform program that looks neither backward to the perpetuation of the liberal social programs nor sideways to the softening of the conservative free-market agenda but forward to a practical vision of the reenergizing of democratic politics and the democratizing of the market economy in America.

CHAPTER 4
INSTITUTIONAL EXPERIMENTS AND AMERICAN HOPES

A major contention of this book is that Americans should use the tools of institutional experimentalism to rethink and rebuild each strand in their religion of possibility: the hope of social opportunity and mobility for the individual; the hope that practical ingenuity can resolve, one by one, the problems people face; and the hope that under democracy individual men and women can achieve the largeness of vision and experience that less democratic civilizations have reserved for the exceptional few. Our message is that unless Americans prove themselves willing to be as open-minded about the institutional arrangements of the country as they have been about almost everything else they will continue to find their hopes frustrated. It is not enough to rebel against the lack of justice unless we also rebel against the lack of imagination.

The structure of society matters to each of the defining American hopes. Practices and institutions make this structure what it is. It is not just the natural result of the many distinct practical constraints Americans have faced in dealing with their problems. Nor is it the expression of an overarching system that would need to be changed, if it could be changed at all, in one fell swoop.

The hope of social mobility—the ability of the determined individual to climb the ladder of class distinctions—depends upon the economic and educational resources at the disposal of each individual as well as upon the barriers of privilege, discrimination, and exclusion he or she must face. For much of their history, Americans have been reluctant to guarantee individuals more than the bare minimum of such resources. They have feared that such an assurance would smother individual responsibility and self-reliance under a heavy blanket of governmental paternalism.

They have sold themselves short. They have failed to understand the many ways in which the bestowal of this basic economic and cultural equipment can be reconciled with a bias toward risk taking, a commitment to competition, and an acknowledgment of the considerable inequalities born of competition. The details of the alternative approaches make all the difference.

The essence of the progressive idea today should lie in the conviction that the advance of the economy toward greater flexibility and decentralization can go hand in hand with a strengthening of individual initiatives and capabilities. Instead of trying to give people something close to tenure in their present jobs, we should seek to assure them the means with which to thrive in the midst of change. Instead of granting a variety of interests—workers, consumers, and local communities as well as business owners—veto power over what businesses do, we should broaden decentralized access to productive resources and opportunities. We should recognize that such a marriage of economic flexibility and individual empowerment can flourish only in the context of a more organized citizenry and a more energized polity than Americans have yet built.

The relation of the core rights and resources every individual should enjoy to the restless experiments of a more vibrant democracy and a more diversified market economy is like the relation between the love a parent gives a child and the willingness of the child to run risks for the sake of transformation and self-transformation. People must be economically and culturally equipped to act as effective citizens and workers. They must also be and feel secure in a haven of protected vital interests if they are to face instability and innovation without fear.

The belief that ordinary men and women can become extraordinary, and find light in the shadowy world of the commonplace—this essential faith of American democracy—depends for its vindication upon the practical arrangements of life in America. We have already remarked that this idea can readily be perverted into a conception of self-salvation that is forgetful of solidarity and intolerant of the raw neediness of human beings, especially of their neediness for one another. That is when the drive for control, power, and distance takes over in the souls of an American men and women.

The search for self-enhancement casts a long shadow in the desperate loneliness that has so often haunted Americans in the midst of their unrivaled capacity for teamwork. Many observers of American life, from the early history of the country to today, have noted the tendency of Americans to inhabit a middle

distance, bathing all social relations in a cheerful imper-
sonal friendliness and standing aloof even while standing together.

It would be foolish to put the sharp pain of human
disconnection entirely down to the practical arrangements of society: Democracy does better at destroying
our illusions about the most intractable causes of human suffering than at destroying those causes themselves. However, democracy also thrives on a moral psychology recognizing that we are embodied spirits and
that the practical circumstances of social life touch even
the most intimate recesses of private experience.

Much in the practical arrangements of American
society turns the social experience of an ordinary
American into a series of those encounters that, according to Madame de Staël, rob us of solitude without
affording us company. In such an experience, people
feel alone even when they work together. They cannot
then achieve the union of self-development and solidarity that has been the great moral dream of their
democracy. By reforming their institutions to expand
opportunities for small-scale social reconstruction, by
making it easier for people to remake their contexts
while doing their jobs, Americans can have a better
chance to realize this dream.

Institutional innovation is equally important to the other element in the American religion of possibility: the habit of problem solving. Americans have traditionally gone about solving problems one at a time. They have been distrustful of the idea that their problems at any given moment fit together into a single scheme. Thus, the temper of American progressive movements has been simple and sincere: majorities against minorities, poor against rich, powerless against powerful. Such a sensibility is impatient with the idea of combined and cumulative institutional change. The obstacles it is willing to recognize are visible: forceful interests rather than hidden assumptions or unchallenged arrangements.

The attitudes of practical progressives are mirrored in the self-image of many a practical politician. The ex-reformer, like the would-be reformer, distrusts, as romantic or dangerous, talk of ideologies, institutional alternatives, and citizens' action. He may see politics as the management of many discrete problems, to be accomplished by patient negotiation with the organized, contradictory interests controlling the national agenda. He may be resigned to low-energy democracy as the only democracy there really is.

The policy discussion permitted by such a mentality takes the established institutions of the country for granted. It is, for that reason, almost incapable of addressing any real social problem. Without ideas about institutional alternatives and without the political mobilization of once passive majorities, politics degenerates into inconclusive bargaining among organized interest groups. Such a politics is incapable of addressing, much less solving, any of the major acknowledged problems of the country. Thus, the antipragmatic pragmatism of the anti-ideological, antimobilizational politicians becomes a self-fulfilling prophecy of the impotence of politics.

When American radicals have broken with the tradition of the sincere progressives and the disillusioned politicians, they have sometimes done so by embracing a view that is equally paralyzing. It is the belief, recommended by European theories like Marxism, in the existence of a system out there—"capitalism," for example—with its driving laws, its inner logic, and its indivisible unity. Either you change the whole system, or you merely try to soften its harsh effects through "reformism." The simple and sincere progressive fails to cross the threshold of questioning and reimagining American institutions, or crosses it only under pressure of extreme crisis and with the help of the collective anxieties and enthusiasms crisis generates. The believer in the idea of the "system" places the institutional arrangements of the country beyond the effective reach of deliberate, piecemeal reconstruction.

We reject the choice between a view that would promote popular interests without reimagining and remaking institutional arrangements and a view that sees such arrangements as pieces of a take-it-or-leave-it system. In the history of modern political ideas and attitudes, the idea of fundamental social change has been associated with the picture of decisive crisis, triggering the total substitution of one way of organizing society by another. The commitment to fragmentary and successive reform—to reform of the laws rather than subversion of the system—has been associated with a repudiation of the idea of discontinuous, structural change.

To understand the truth about political possibility, we need to jumble these categories up, combining the idea of step-by-step reform with the idea that institutions matter. We have it in our power to reimagine and remake them. The institutions of a society are its fate. Transformative politics is, like art, an anti-fate, restoring to us a freedom we had renounced or forgotten.

Because we propose here many connected reforms in many areas of social life, some readers may feel dispirited by the sense that nothing can be accomplished unless everything is achieved at once. It is a false impression, a legacy of the old idea of the indivisible system, which exists on a take-it-or-leave-it basis. The path of reform can begin from any of the starting points we describe; circumstance and opportunity will decide which. We can then advance along one of these fronts for a certain distance before we hit limits. We cannot then cross those limits without advancing on some of the other fronts.

Again, if we propose a reform that seems distant from present realities and debates, people may say: interesting but utopian. If we propose a reform close to the established situation, people may respond: feasible but trivial. Thus, all proposals may seem either trivial or utopian. Why bother? It is a false dilemma arising from a mistake about the nature of programmatic ideas.

A program such as ours is not a blueprint; it begins to map out a path. The steps along the way can and should be described both at points close to present circumstances and at points further away. The direction—and its effect upon people's understanding of their interests and identities as well as upon their practical problems—is what matters. Only when we fail to hold in our minds a credible view of social change do we fall back on a fake, surrogate standard of political realism:

that a proposal is realistic according to its closeness to what exists.

It is easy to be a realist when you accept everything. It is easy to be a visionary when you confront nothing. To accept little and confront much, and to do so on the basis of an informed vision of piecemeal but cumulative change, is the way and the solution.

American progressives have fought to keep the American religion of possibility alive by lifting the twin burdens of class and racial oppression upon American democracy. Waves of progressivism have promoted the rights and well-being of workers, people of color, women, the disabled, and others excluded from the bounty of American society. To a lesser extent, progressives have struggled against the narrow-minded ethic of individual self-improvement in the name of a larger vision of the unbreakable ties between individual self-reliance and social solidarity. They have been least clear-sighted and successful in confronting and lifting the third limit to the religion of possibility: the anti-experimentalist attitude toward the institutional arrangements of the United States. Such a confrontation is precisely what American progressivism must achieve today if it is to address the unresolved problems of the country.

CHAPTER 5
THE FRUSTRATION OF AMERICAN DEMOCRACY

There is broad consensus in the United States about what the basic problems of the country are. The economy has failed to achieve growth in productivity that is either inclusive of all citizens or rapid enough (although there are signs that productivity has recently begun both to rise more quickly and to do so in more sectors of business). The innovative practices of the best firms—the turning of production into permanent innovation—have remained within a relatively iso-

lated, advanced part of the economy. Formidable levels
of public and private debt have amassed; the measure of
domestic saving in the United States is low; and the
country consequently depends upon the purchase of its
public debt and the use of its domestic currency by foreigners. Vast wealth, privilege, and power have accumulated in the hands of a tiny and self-serving corporate
elite, which pays itself proportionately more—and pays
workers proportionately less—than in any other industrial democracy. The present systems of education and
health care impose a burden on growth and prosperity
as well as upon social welfare. These systems are, at their
best, preeminent in the world. They nevertheless abandon a large part of the American people to inferior education or deficient care. For what they omit as well as
for what they provide, they exact from the country a
terrible price.

There is also wide agreement about the problems in
social policy and social life. The country has seen increasing inequality of wealth and income, driving the life
chances of individuals apart (even though the influence
of inherited class advantage upon these life chances may
have diminished in the top if not in the bottom half of
the class system). The extraordinary hierarchy and seg-
mentation of education and health care juxtaposes the

best and the worst in the world of industrial democracies and abandons millions to ignorance, incapacity, and anxiety, when not to disease and death. The contrast between the considerable entitlements of the old and the defunding of the young is extreme and insane, with the result that children swell the ranks of the poor in the United States. Racial injustice and racial resentment continue to pervade many aspects of American life. There seem to be flaws in both approaches—one that seeks to deal with race now, the better to deal with class later, and another that insists upon addressing both at the same time, connecting them, for example, in the redesign of affirmative action programs. Present arrangements perpetuate a predominantly black, Latino, and Native American underclass—poor, uneducated, and, save for their religious life, desperate and disorganized. Family life in this underclass is deranged, with children depending upon single mothers and young males resigned in overwhelming numbers to a life of violence, drugs, joblessness, and imprisonment, at war with a society that has first abandoned and then condemned them rather than condemning itself for this abandonment. The weakening throughout American life of many of the forms of voluntary association—engagement in families, unions, fraternal orders, parent-teacher associations, churches, and clubs—upon which the country so heavily relied produces the sense of isolation, loneliness, and powerlessness from which so many Americans suffer. (A large percentage of the American people declare in polls that they have no friends, and one in three Americans lives alone.) Millions of Americans surrender to drink and drugs or to a popular culture specializing in fantasies of empowerment that offer a temporary escape from the boredom and humiliations of humdrum, daily life.

In politics, where solutions must begin, there is less agreement about the sources of trouble. Progressives, if not yet many of their fellow Americans, see the following problems. Money and monied interests exert an inordinate influence upon the outcome of elections and the direction of policy. The judiciary has often sanctified this influence as if the ability of money to talk, magnifying the voices of a few and crowding out the voices of the many, were a principle rather than a wrong. Public campaign financing that would counterbalance the political power of money is lacking. We have failed to provide free access to television and to understand that almost all of the evils of television in politics can be reversed by simply guaranteeing more television time to the views in contest. The political parties and their capacity to serve as the authors and agents of clearly defined alternatives have weakened, encouraged by the pseudodemocratic system of primaries. Popular disinterest in politics is widespread, manifest in the refusal of half of the electorate to vote, one of the lowest levels of civic engagement of any democracy, rich or poor. The most talented individuals are unwilling even to consider the possibility of a political career, or, when they consider it, to face the hustling for money that all but the very rich must undertake. Those who have won elective office readily abandon it for whatever more exciting or lucrative opportunity comes up, while the country accepts this degraded view of political office with equanimity. In an era of relative world peace and skepticism about activist government the American presidency has shrunk. The Congress absorbs itself in short-term service to constituents and funders. Progressives make self-defeating attempts to use judicial power to circumvent the consequences of their setbacks in national politics. Recent conservative administrations have succeeded in convincing Americans that they have little to hope for from the government or from political work. The progressive forces, in and outside the Democratic party, have willingly resigned themselves to the humanization of the Republican agenda as the outer limit of their transformative ambitions. The politically active minority of the country generally agrees that this surrender is the straightforward expression of political realism rather than the self-fulfilling consequence of a failure of ideas and of nerve.

Yet the country that suffers from all these problems shows irresistible energy in its culture and social life. It is a country with a thousand little Silicon Valleys, where a new logic of practical collaboration and restless experimentalism is emerging in countless businesses and schools: a logic subordinating routine to innovation, tearing down barriers between conception and execution, and combining individual initiative with teamwork. Though narrowly focused on economic gain and tainted by social exclusion, such islands of energetic experimentalism show a capability that needs to be made available to many more people and applied to many more problems. The public life of the United States fails to do justice to this astonishing vitality; its poverty of people, practices, and ideas is a failure that seems both unnecessary and undeserved.

The advanced forms of practical experimentalism may have little need of government to flourish in a favored and isolated sector of the economy. They cannot, however, spread to broader segments of American society without help. The task of American progressivism today is to create a public life supportive of this vitality that channels it in a democratic direction without sacrificing independent initiative to a centralizing bureaucracy. The first step in this direction is to understand better the unresolved and unrecognized dilemmas underlying the admitted problems of the country.

Throughout the history of the United States, Americans in general, and American progressives in particular, have oscillated between two ideas of social progress through economic reform, without being able fully to embrace either. From Thomas Jefferson's vision of a yeoman republic of small farmers, to Wendell Phillips's forty acres and a mule for black ex-slaves, to small business against big business, decentralized power resonates in the American imagination. Carried far enough to matter, such an approach has always seemed to many Americans, especially powerful ones, too restrictive of both economic efficiency and cultural complexity.

The alternative to the entrenchment of small business has been a national scheme of redistribution implemented by the federal government. Although Americans have, since the establishment of the progressive income tax in 1913, accepted something of this alternative and clung to it even in periods of reaction against progressivism, they have never been willing to go as far as Europeans, who accept much heavier taxation. They have feared the suppression of self-reliance and enterprise. They have been unwilling to jeopardize, even at the cost of greater social inequality, social exclusion, and social cruelty, the bottom-up energy that has been the strength of America.

Breaking through this dilemma demands institutional innovations. It requires the use of politics to reshape governmental and economic arrangements in ways that escape the stereotypes of entrenched ideologies. Here, however, another dilemma of American politics emerges to cloud insight and inhibit action. Americans have always wavered between the idea that they have to keep reinventing themselves and their arrangements to make good on the promises of American freedom, and the contrary idea that they have already found the basic design of a free society. When faced with economic disaster or military jeopardy, they have awakened to the imperatives of national politics. When such perils have seemed under control, they have derided national politics as a barely respectable sideshow to their personal responsibilities. Only in moments of deep crisis—the Civil War, the Great Depression, the civil uprisings in the 1960s—have Americans pursued national politics with democratic, innovative energy. Private enterprise and charity may seem incapable of solving many problems, but political action in the form of governmental programs has usually seemed to Americans to create as many problems as it solves.

Americans must resolve their ambivalence about politics if they are to fashion the institutional improvements that would allow them to solve the admitted problems of the country, and begin to address the major feature of the emerging world economy that has made many of these problems both more urgent and more intractable.

CHAPTER 6
VANGUARDS AND REARGUARDS IN THE NEW WORLD ECONOMY

People used to think that production was distributed hierarchically in the world. Advanced production—with large-scale investment, fancy machines, and highly skilled labor—takes place in the rich economies. More backward production—with less money invested per worker, more primitive technology, and low or moderately skilled labor—goes on in the poorer, developing countries. This idea may seem almost self-evidently true. It has nevertheless become increasingly false. Advanced production takes place today throughout the world: in Brazil, India, or Indonesia as well as in the United States, Germany, and Japan. The driving force of the world economy has become a worldwide network of productive vanguards, exchanging people, practices, and ideas as well as goods, services, and capital. The vaunted and exaggerated mobility of capital works in the service of this worldwide network when it does not amount to a speculative sideshow to the main action.

The kernel of the new economic vanguardism that has spread throughout the world lies less in deep investment and pioneering technology than in turning production into a practice of continuous learning and permanent innovation. Such a practice depends upon skills. However, the most important of these skills concerns society rather than technology: skill at cooperative innovation, loosening the restraints that any established set of roles and relations imposes upon experimental novelty.

In each country, rich or poor, the vanguard remains separated from the rearguard. This separation has become the fundamental source of social inequality and exclusion. In rich countries like the Scandinavian social democracies, a comprehensive, redistributive welfare state muffles the unequalizing consequences of the division between vanguard and rearguard. In rich countries like the United States, the weaker and more selective character of redistributive social programs lets the division between vanguard and rearguard operate more unrestrictedly. In poor countries like India, the effects of the gap between vanguard and rearguard are moderated less by redistributive social programs than by the politically supported diffusion of small-scale property, especially family agriculture. In poor countries like Brazil, the weakness of both small property and social programs allows the contrast between vanguard and rearguard to work unchecked.

The two devices available for softening the social consequences of the contrast—redistributive social policy and the support for traditional small business—suffer from the same defect. They lack an intimate connection with the central logic of economic innovation and growth in a world where the network of productive vanguards plays the commanding role.

The fateful programmatic question is whether we can hope to overcome, however gradually, the contrast between vanguard and rearguard, or whether we must resign ourselves merely to moderate its consequences. The chastened and disoriented progressives who have surrendered to the humanization of the inevitable—like the American Democrats whose program has become a softened version of the program of their Republican adversaries—have answered this question one way. American progressives must answer it another way, if they are to keep the American religion of possibility alive and begin solving the practical problems of the country.

The extension of vanguardist practices beyond the favored sectors of society where they now flourish and the consequent lifting of the backward sectors require help, including help from the government. The rearguard will not be able to lift itself by its bootstraps. The task is to give this help in a way respecting the economic discipline and the decentralized insight of a market rather than imposing a bureaucratic scheme of favors and privileges.

In at least one area of the American economy, in historical perspective, this goal was carried out to tremendous effect. American agriculture, from the nineteenth-century Homestead Acts up to the New Deal–era agricultural extension services and credit unions, was organized as a partnership between the federal government and the family farmer. The Homestead Act of 1862 promised 160 acres of relatively free land to citizens who intended to make it productive. The New Deal provided support to protect and encourage farmers to yield high levels of productivity. If now much of the traditional apparatus of this partnership seems archaic, restrictive, and ridden with unjustifiable concessions to powerful interests, we must not forget that it worked for much of the history of the country. It laid the basis for an agriculture combining remarkable efficiency with widespread decentralization of economic power and initiative. The domination of big business over industry found a partial counterweight in an economy of family farms and small towns. What the American progressives never discovered was an effective counterpart to this agrarian alliance between the little guy and the government that could work beyond agriculture, for the rest of the economy. Nor did they envisage the political reforms that would sustain and organize the high-energy popular politics needed to support such a project over time.

CHAPTER 7

THE RECENT PAST OF AMERICAN PROGRESSIVISM

With what resources today can American progressivism confront the admitted problems of the country and renew the American religion of possibility? The last great moment of progressive inspiration and renovation was Roosevelt's New Deal. The lasting legacy of the New Deal, beyond the particular federal programs it produced, was an idea of social citizenship. Confronted with the economic crisis of the 1930s, Americans would not allow themselves to be abandoned to the supposedly spontaneous workings of a market that had ceased adequately to function. They would demand that the government rescue them from an economic disablement that denied them the means of self-reliance. They would not content themselves with Hoover's invocation of a free economic and political order. They would use the powers of government to ensure the effectiveness of individual and collective self-determination. Nor would they count solely on private charity—glorified as "voluntarism"—to change a condition of widespread despair. They were citizens of a democracy, and they would insist upon giving their citizenship a content that was real because it was social. As the business interests were brought to accept the practical consequences of the idea of social citizenship, the government, for all the rhetorical thundering of the progressives, renounced any attack on the essentials of corporate power in America. In this compromise lay the basic terms of the New Deal settlement, the American counterpart to what social democrats had begun to achieve in Europe.

The point was not merely to "regulate" the market or to strike a "balance" between markets and rights, as the unimaginative and unconscious conservatism of a later era would have it. It was to change the institutional arrangements defining a market economy. It was to democratize the market economy. Similarly, when in earlier periods the federal and state governments had formed a partnership with the family farmer to establish the most successful and efficient agriculture in the world, while giving millions of people the tools for practical independence, the result had not been the displacement of the market by governmental command. It had been a different kind of market economy in agriculture than would otherwise have emerged: one more supportive of both decentralized economic initiative and vigorous democratic life.

As the New Deal years went on, the early tinkering with the arrangements that defined the market economy and shaped the dealings between business and government gave way to an emphasis upon minimal guarantees against extreme economic insecurity, especially for the elderly; the more equal diffusion of opportunities for consumption; and the moderation of the business cycle. Wartime experiments with economic reorganization came to be seen as the requirement of a passing emergency. In peacetime, deviance from conventional forms of the market economy would be confined to quarantined sectors of economic life, like the defense procurements industry, where a mixed form of public-private planning of production has continued to thrive to this very day. Only a residue of the early institutional ambitions remained, in the form of a halfhearted commitment to defend against big business the rights of organized labor and of the American worker.

The decline and confinement of tinkering with the market economy to make it more democratic presaged the later history of the New Deal settlement in American politics. There were retreats and advances. Whereas the retreats seem, from today's disillusioned perspective, to have been inescapable, the advances appear either precarious or ineffective.

The Democratic party—ever the party of the progressives—has withdrawn from any attempt to treat the present distribution of economic power and advantage in the country as an alterable circumstance rather than an inexorable fate. It has abandoned the effort to increase, through strengthened labor rights, the take of wages from national income. Many factors have contributed to the retreat: the demoralizing experience of the stagflation of the 1970s, the embarrassments of European social democracy with its high levels of unemployment, the newfound freedom of capital to cross borders, the comparatively low tax yield in the United States as well as the dependence of American public finance upon the purchase of Treasury obligations by foreigners, and the unchallenged intellectual authority of reactionary economic ideas—taking as dogma the self-defeating character of policies intended to trump the capital markets or to make wages grow more rapidly than productivity gains.

Remember the pundits and gurus of the Democratic party. Twenty years ago, they spoke of "industrial policy" and the defense of organized labor. Then they switched to talking vaguely about governmental investment in people and in the transport and communication network of the country. Then, with Clinton's accession to power, they discarded that timid refrain, and resigned themselves to balancing the books, currying favor with the bond market, and promoting good feelings, as opposed to substantive justice, among the races.

Despite the current retreat, two great advances took place in the generations following the New Deal. The first advance was the launching, during Johnson's presidency, of a second wave of entitlement programs addressed to the poor, superimposed upon Roosevelt's programs, directed to the broad working majority of the country (the "middle class"). The second advance was the development, by an alliance among the civil rights movement, the Democratic party in power, and the federal judiciary, of a far-reaching body of civil rights law, written to stamp out the evils of racial and sexual discrimination and racist segregation. The trouble is that, disconnected from any broader effort to promote democratization of the market, curtail corporate power, and energize democratic politics, each of these two advances has proved fragile to the point of being reversible. Each has turned out inadequate to its professed objectives.

Those who proposed to wage war against poverty found themselves reduced to helping the poor, without having the tools that would make such help effective. They lacked both the wit and the power to challenge any of the economic and educational arrangements that imposed deep divisions between advanced and backward sectors of the economy and between the life paths that led to each. With middle-class entitlement programs like Social Security and Medicare so cleanly separated, by the accident of their historical evolution and legislative design, from poverty assistance programs, and with a country in which the federal government seemed increasingly powerless to relieve the problems of ordinary working families, many lost patience with policies that at best alleviated some consequences of poverty rather than addressing its causes. They believed those schemes to be funded at the expense of the working majority rather than of the sanctimonious elite and the monied interests.

Those who saw the struggle against racial discrimination as the first step in a longer and larger campaign against racial injustice discovered that antidiscrimination and antisegregation laws, rigidly separated from the problems of economic opportunity and inequality, produce effects that are real but limited. In some key ways, these effects are as dangerous as they are useful. Racial discrimination has diminished in every realm of American life and every region of the United States since the age of Jim Crow, especially the South. Blacks have been joined by Latinos and other marginalized groups in their struggle and their advancement. A black bourgeoisie has grown and begun to prosper.

However, the benefits of the antidiscrimination programs have been enjoyed in inverse proportion to need, reaching the black professional and business class more than the black working class, and the black working class more than the black underclass. The situation of this underclass remains catastrophic, and no antidiscrimination piety will improve it. The majority of poor blacks has become increasingly alienated from its leaders, the educated black minority, which has for the most part been accommodated, coopted, and even feted by the elite institutions of the country. This process threatens to repeat itself among Latinos and others.

The present form of affirmative action, sitting uneasily between aggressive antidiscrimation and race-based preferment in employment and education, has fueled resentments in the white small-business and working classes. These resentments in turn help prevent the emergence of a transracial progressive majority. The absence of such a majority makes the present limitations of policy for the redress of racial injustice seem inescapable, thus closing a circle that squeezes American democracy dry. A balkanized citizenry cannot reach a progressive consensus on this issue, especially when awareness of class is buried in the fray.

The Democratic party and the progressive movement forged by this sequence of striking retreats and precarious advances has two factions. One, smaller faction looks back nostalgically to the New Deal. This group clings to a cause in whose further advance it gives no real sign of believing. The other, larger faction, which includes Clinton and Gore, as it included Carter before them, looks sideways to the Republican party. It hopes to humanize what it no longer seeks to rival or replace. It finds its view of the world confirmed in the story line of the most prestigious newspapers and magazines and

in the myopic pronouncements of the academic econo-
mists and policy experts.

This is a rump and a residue rather than a party or
a movement. Its leaders pride themselves on being man-
agers rather than ideologists. They speak and act as if the
government of a country were like the management of a
business—and an old-fashioned business at that, one
satisfied with balancing the books, keeping the workers
disciplined, and animating them with pep talks. However, the paradoxical result of their antipragmatic pragmatism is to make politics seem largely irrelevant to the
solution of any of the recognized problems of the country. Such a pragmatism will backfire soon.

Our politicians deny themselves and their fellow
citizens the ability to experiment with the institutional
arrangements of the American economy and American
democracy. They resign themselves to brokering legislative deals among the powerful organized interests while
calling upon voluntary social action to save the country
from the incapacity of the government over which they
preside. They claim to be practical, yet seem forever unable to deliver the goods. Thus arises, in the United States
today, an oppressive contrast between the vitality and
greatness of the country and the littleness and deadness
of its public life.

CHAPTER 8
AMERICAN PROGRESSIVISM REORIENTED

The work of American progressivism today is to democratize the market economy and energize representative democracy. Progressives should build the link between economic reforms designed to challenge the stark divisions between vanguards and rearguards, and political reforms intended to quicken democratic politics in America.

The program we outline opposes dualism, the division of the economy into a rigid contrast of advanced and backward sectors, and proposes a deepening of democracy: strengthening the tools for the collective discussion and solution of collective problems. It is, therefore, a productivist program, rooting a bias toward more equality of income and wealth in a set of economic arrangements and a strategy of economic growth, rather than merely attempting, through retrospective and compensatory tax-and-transfer, to undo part of what the economy has wrought. It rejects the simple contrast between governmental activism and free enterprise, not because it wants to have a little of each, but because it insists upon having more of both. To this end, our program offers to renovate the institutional machinery for a decentralized and experimental partnership between government and business. It seeks to extend the rights of labor, increasing the wage take from national income. The point is to do so in ways that serve the interests of the working people of the country as a whole rather than benefit the relatively privileged and organized workers in capital- and technology-rich industries. It goes beyond the fight against racial discrimination to the redress of racial injustice while recognizing that the prob-

lems of racial injustice are inseparable from the problems of class injustice. Our program defends a refinanc-
ing of the government on a basis that reconciles a high
tax yield—and therefore a more effective governmental
ability to invest in people's capabilities—with the need
to preserve, indeed to strengthen, incentives to work,
save, and invest. It both exemplifies and encourages the
master practice of democratic experimentalism: motivated, sustained, and cumulative tinkering with the institutional arrangements of the government and the
economy. It relies on a more engaged and informed citizenry rather than on a more enlightened technocratic
elite. And it maps out the steps that make possible the
gradual emergence of a lasting transracial progressive
majority in American politics as both the condition and
the consequence of the democratizing changes it proposes. It is not the humanization of the inevitable; it is
the alternative to an unnecessary and unacceptable fate.
It is the American religion of possibility translated into a
plan for the next step.

A key assumption of this proposal is that the focus of
ideological controversy and institutional innovation
throughout the world has shifted. The old conflict between market and command, progovernment and anti-

government, is dead or dying. The days of pitting state planning against laissez-faire policies are over. They are giving way to a new contest between the alternative institutional forms of representative democracies, market economies, and free civil societies. The institutional arrangements for political, economic, and social pluralism now established in the North Atlantic world will turn out to be a subset of a larger set of institutional and social possibilities. We must now look to a democratic civilization that embraces new ways of organizing and deepening political, economic, and social freedom.

Institutions house civilizations. Ideals live in practices. By pursuing divergent institutional pathways, according to their own needs and strivings, countries will reveal the vital role of national distinctions in a world of democracies: to develop the powers and possibilities of humanity in different directions. The United States—the most experimentalist of modern nations—has the most to gain, spiritually as well as practically, from this rebirth of its religion of human possibility on a global scale. The doctrine of the one true way flatters the country, and betrays it.

Here are some of the planks in a progressive platform faithful to these ambitions. They are meant to mark a path rather than to define a blueprint. Each of their elements is controversial. Each element could be replaced by equivalent devices. Taken together, they nevertheless indicate a way to begin from where we are now. From this point close by, the path can lead, by small, incremental steps, into a society that is both more democratic and more innovative. In that society the grid of class, gender, and race weighs less heavily upon our life in common.

TAXES: FROM LIBERAL PIETIES TO REDISTRIBUTIVE REALITIES

The United States has the lowest aggregate tax take of any of the major industrial countries: the revenues of the federal government amount to 20 percent of GDP and the revenues of all three levels of American government to 36 percent GDP (as contrasted, for example, with 47 percent of GDP in France in a recent year). A considerable body of evidence shows that people in many countries support a high tax base tenaciously as long as its improved social, educational, and health benefits are palpable. To be sure, we must not kill the goose that lays the golden eggs, dampening incentives to work, save, and invest. One solution may be to reform taxation so that it falls on consumption rather than on income.

Progressives regularly oppose consumption taxes,

particularly when they apply to transactions (as in a sales tax) rather than to individuals. Such taxes are admittedly regressive because they hit the poor proportionately more than the rich. Business interests, for the same reason, favor them. The business interests and the progressives are both mistaken. The most important lesson of comparative tax experience of first-world nations is that redistribution takes place much more on the spending side of of the budget than on its revenue-raising side. In other words, it matters less how fair the raising of revenue is than how much the government takes if it can use what it takes to help the people who most need help. The United States has on paper one of the most progressive tax systems in the industrialized world, and the greatest levels of social and economic inequality. Despairing of a political economy that would achieve real redistribution, American progressives today prefer to genuflect to progressive pieties than to achieve progressive results.

Broad-based taxation of consumption (as through the so-called comprehensive, flat-rate, value-added tax) can make it possible to increase revenues while easing the burden of taxation upon saving and investment. It is a money machine. In a second stage, once tax reform has secured the basis of a strong revenue flow, friendly to economic growth, we can begin to give a larger role to two sets of redistributive taxes. One would be the direct taxation, on a steeply progressive scale, of what an individual spends on his own consumption with a basic level of spending left untaxed—like an income tax with an exemption for saving. The other would be taxes on the accumulation of wealth and on its transmission through family inheritance and family gifts.

American democracy should work toward the generalization of a principle of social inheritance. Everyone should be able to count on a minimum of resources. These resources are the tools of self-reliance, not an alternative to self-reliance. People should have a social-endowment account so that society can do for everyone a little bit of what family inheritance does for a few. At major moments in their lives—when they go to college, make a down payment on a house, or open a business—they should be able to draw on this account. The minimum account should increase according to two countervailing principles: compensation for special need or handicap according to predefined criteria, and reward for special capacity, competitively demonstrated.

PENSIONS, SAVING, AND INVESTMENT:
THE RESOURCES FOR GROWTH

Capital is now supposed to be globalized. It is not: The truth is that only a small portion of investment funds crosses national frontiers, and in doing so sometimes makes a big ruckus. The architects of the new, neoliberal world economy are building, in the name of economic freedom, an order that allows capital to roam all over the globe, and imprisons labor in the nation-state. Most capital nevertheless stays at home.

For a long time, the United States has fallen into the habit of depending upon other people's money: foreigners put their money in the United States, buy the public debt of the American government, and even hold—abroad—most of the paper currency. Like many pieces of undeserved good fortune, this one has its dark side. It helps keep the United States from facing the full consequences, or recognizing the full dimensions, of its low saving level. Gross domestic saving in the United States is 15 percent of GDP, well below what it is in many other rich economies. Dependence upon foreign saving limits the freedom of maneuver in American economic policy and makes economic growth in America hostage to events in other parts of the world.

The need to raise the level of saving in order to ensure sustained economic progress is an opportunity as well as a problem. For it can help push the country in a direction in which it has other reasons to travel. It provides a context in which to reconcile faster economic growth with a more equal distribution of national wealth.

A shift to consumption-based taxation may help raise the saving level by exempting saving from taxation as well as by helping the federal government avoid future deficits. However, the greatest, because most direct, boost to saving is likely to come from a system for the public organization of compulsory private saving. The most important setting in which to introduce such a system is Social Security and private-pension reform. The United States hardly needs the astronomical saving rate (51 percent) that tiny Singapore has achieved under an unnecessarily bureaucratic and centralized version of such a system of required private saving. All it needs is to do better, socially as well as economically, than it has.

The law would require everyone to save in special pension funds a certain percentage of their incomes, defined on a progressive scale according to income levels. Middle-level income earners would keep what they get.

High earners would have some of what they save redistributed away from them into the accounts of low earners. Low earners, demonstrating either that they work or that they suffer from a problem that prevents them from working, would have money distributed into their accounts (simply an extension of the principal of the earned-income tax credit, which long enjoyed bipartisan support).

The money would be paid into a broad range of independently managed and competitive funds—not just conventional mutual funds, investing in the established equity and bond markets, but mixed public-private venture-capital funds, investing in new business. Many of these venture-capital funds would be chartered to invest in a diversified mix of start-up firms, and some would get matching or contributory funds, or credit enhacements, from government to invest in the small and medium-sized businesses of the economic rearguard. Once fully developed, such a system would replace both social security and private pensions.

Is this proposal a pay-as-you-go redistributive pension scheme like Social Security? Or a get-what-you-saved saving scheme like private pensions? It combines the market orientation of the latter with the equalizing commitments of the former. Is it a marginal improvement to the existing conduit between saving and productive investment offered by banks and stock markets? Or is it the beginning of an attempt to build, alongside banks and stock markets, an additional bridge between saving and productive investment? We cannot tell beforehand, and it hardly matters.

In the United States, as in other industrial economies, an average of 80 percent of investment in production by businesses of all sizes comes from "retained earnings," what companies save from profits. Most of what individuals save disappears into a financial casino, a money-filled black hole with haphazard, uneven relevance to the funding of production and innovation. Venture capital—the financing of new enterprise by outside investors—remains a tiny sideshow to the operations of this casino. In the spirit of democratic experimentalism, we should try to find a way to tap more of the productive potential of saving by innovating in the economic arrangements that make saving available to enterprise. We should do so in ways that help anchor, in the core institutions of the economy, a bias toward greater equality of access and greater freedom of initiative.

CHILDREN AND EDUCATION: THE FUTURE FIRST

The top priority of social legislation in the United States today, and the greatest justification for a high tax take, should be child protection. The law must ensure food, medical, and dental support through families or neighborhoods to every child who needs them.

Thirty-eight percent of poor people in the United States are children. The contrast between the relative generosity for the old—through Social Security and Medicare—and the cruel and stupid abandonment of the young is one of the great injustices of American life. Frustration with the results of programs like Aid to Families with Dependent Children has now prompted Democrats to join with Republicans in broadening what was already a tremendous gap.

Experience throughout the world has taught us that such support is more effective when families and community groups share in the formulation as well as the implementation of programs, turning public-resource transfers into devices of social solidarity and triggers for social organization. A parent movement that enables the nurturers of our society to come through for their children is a good start. The partnership of a weakened family with a welfare bureaucracy falls short. It must be backed up, and transformed, by the action of neighborhood associations and family networks. Cooperative, supervised preschooling and after-school care can form part of their job.

Social supports for children can serve as the front line in the development of social rights for everyone. For example, the sensible and characteristically American way to introduce universal, publicly backed health insurance would be to begin by guaranteeing health insurance to all children. In the setting of child support, we could try out different mixes of public funding and private payment, of public oversight and private management. The successful models in universal health insurance for children could then be extended, by incremental steps, to the adult population.

The child crisis converges with the failure of the American public school system to accomplish a central part of the mission of schools in a democracy: to rescue the child from the limitations of its class and family situation, giving it access to a world of longer memory, broader imagination, and stronger ambition. The professional and business class avoids this failure either by living in upscale neighborhoods, with better than average public schools, or by sending their children to private schools. The majority of public schools become both a source and a mirror of social apartheid in America. This crisis is not the inevitable price of political and economic freedom; it is simply the result of bad arrangements, bad ideas, and bad politics.

With the strengthening of a national focus upon the future, and therefore upon children, we can address anew the reform of public education. Three principles should guide our efforts.

The first principle is that, in a democracy, the child must be available to the school; it is not enough for the school to be available to the child. To exercise effectively the right to a public education, children need ample support, if necessary, from the government, and, if possible, in their families.

The second principle is that everyone should master a core set of generic conceptual and practical skills, getting ready for a life of instability, learning, and innovation. Specialized study and vocational training should supplement rather than replace education in these basic, multipurpose skills. What begins in childhood should extend throughout life in the form of continuing adult education.

The third principle is that, if democracy is to triumph, localism in education should be contained. Schools should be able to rely upon state and national as well as local finance so that they do not reproduce the economic advantages and disadvantages of their communities. Nor should their curricula passively reflect community attitudes. If parent participation is important, so is the role of the school as a counterweight to the limitations of local opinion and family circumstance.

The school in a democracy should take no part in delivering to the child the ancient message of the family or the local community: Become like me. It has a bigger job: to equip the child with the means to think and to stand on his or her own feet, bringing the ideas and experiences of far away or long ago to bear upon the understanding and the criticism of the here and now. The school should examine possibilities of imagination and of life that the surrounding society is unable or unwilling to countenance. It should be the voice of the future—of alternative futures—within the present, and it should recognize in the child, the future worker and citizen, a little prophet.

Thus, we need to prevent any one level of government, and any one form of connection among school, community, and family, from having the definitive say over what goes on in the classroom. A system of multiple accountability, multiple guidance, and multiple funding—from federal, state, and municipal levels of government—will help liberate the public schools from exclusive dependence upon local control and give them the economic and cultural resources with which to form free people.

RACIAL DISCRIMINATION AND CLASS INJUSTICE: HOW NOT TO FORGET ABOUT ONE WHILE DEALING WITH THE OTHER

Racial antagonisms hurt American democracy twice: first by the evils of racial discrimination and segregation; and, second, by the obstacles they create to the redress of class injustice. Working Americans remain divided by race, struggling under the injustices of racial oppression and resentful of what often seem to be the unjust effects of policies designed to right racial wrongs. These divisions have helped keep them from uniting around leaders, organizations, policies, and programs committed to loosen the constraints that class status imposes on the life chances of individuals. The present body of antidiscrimination law and policy—including affirmative action—has become both part of the solution and part of the problem.

The flaw in the conventional approach to racial discrimination and affirmative action today is that it sits uncomfortably between two missions, accomplishing neither fully and making the execution of the one seem a hindrance to the achievement of the other. One goal is the struggle against racial discrimination; the other is the improvement of the circumstances of a racially marked underclass.

The legal and political triumphs of the civil rights movement, in and outside government, have succeeded in diminishing the force of racial discrimination throughout American life. It would be perverse to belittle this achievement. Nevertheless, the antidiscrimination law we now have may be too little to combat the hardened, substantial forms of racial prejudice that remain. In some areas—affirmative action first among them—established law and practice go beyond antidiscrimination to some element of active preferment in jobs and education in favor of blacks and other groups that continue to suffer from racial oppression. However, law and practice move toward this goal without either reaching or acknowledging it; the majority of the country and its jurists reject a policy of race-based compensatory privileges. In the meantime, however, this confused, halfhearted policy produces some benefits—captured disproportionately by the elites of the favored groups (the black professional and business class, for example)—and countless resentments—felt by the white losers, real or imagined. These resentments help prevent the development of the transracial progressive majority we need.

The solution is to cut boldly through this tangle of inhibiting confusions, clearly distinguishing antidiscrimination from the larger effort to redress the difficult mixture of racial and class injustice—and devising means suited to each of these two objectives.

Progressives should confront racial discrimination as a distinct evil. They should persuade Americans to follow the example of some other countries, criminalizing its most serious instances. At the same time we should insist upon creating many more situations in American life where people of different races work, study, and live together, discovering in their human individualities likenesses and differences that cut across racial divisions. Now that there is disappointment with the cause of racial desegregation, the case for pressing it as a tonic to American democracy has never been stronger.

The suffering of a black and Latino underclass that combines racial stigma with class subjugation presents a different problem, requiring different solutions. We do need a policy of active preferment in education and jobs in favor of those caught in entrenched situations of social disadvantage and exclusion from which they cannot

escape, readily or at all, by their own initiative. However, we should not base this preferment solely on race,
for race is typically just one element, although often a
major one, of the social disablement we seek to repair.

The law should develop standards to give a special
push in schooling and employment—and therefore also
in admissions and hirings—to those who suffer from an
accumulation of forms of disadvantage from which they
cannot be expected to escape on their own. Prominent
among these sources of subjugation are class, race, gender, and handicap. We know for a fact that it is the con-
vergence of some of these factors in the life situation of
an individual that may prevent him or her from seizing
upon the opportunities of American society. Placed in
this context, the offer of preferment loses its invidious,
narrowly racial character. We can defend it, as a matter
of the law and the Constitution (although it would
surely require a change of present constitutional under-
standings), because it helps make feasible the demand
for individual self-reliance. It helps keep the promise of
equal opportunity for all.

Such an effort is useful and even necessary. It is,
however, no substitute for the broader attempt to democratize the market economy in America, narrowing
the gap between vanguard and rearguard. We must take

it for what it is: a subsidiary tool of social policy but a major vindication of justice for the individual.

ECONOMIC VANGUARDISM OUTSIDE THE VANGUARD: NARROWING THE GAP BETWEEN THE ADVANCED AND BACKWARD SECTORS OF THE ECONOMY

The most important issue of political economy today in the United States, as throughout the world, is not deficits, taxes, saving, or even, in the conventional sense, jobs. It is the social form that will be taken by a way of working together and producing goods and services that is beginning to reconstruct economies all over the globe. A method of collaboration rather than a technology of production lies at the heart of this advanced economy, although technologies of information and communication have helped equip it. It is a method of flattened hierarchies and permanent innovation, of fluid job definitions and constant reshaping of products, services, and practices. It combines teamwork with competition. It is production as learning. It can be carried out by decentralized big businesses, or by cooperative-competitive networks of small and medium-sized businesses. It thrives under particular conditions: a background of community life and good government, especially good local government—able to ensure high-quality basic education, opportunities for continuous reskilling, dense networks of association, and the high trust such networks breed—as well as first-rate transport and communication facilities. It is not just for making computers and software or for supplying highly paid professional services; it is for doing anything. Flexible, high-technology, and knowledge-rich production is here to stay.

Where such conditions are largely present, national government can take a back seat. Without intervention, economic vanguardism flourishes in an isolated, advantaged part of the economy. That is the situation we see emerging in America as elsewhere: a world of advanced sectors and regions connected with one another and weakly linked to the backward sectors and regions of their own societies.

The reordering of production as learning will happen one way or another. The crucial issue is whether it will happen in forms that are more or less socially inclusive. The work of progressives must be to steer it in an inclusive direction. To that end, we need to fashion the instruments for decentralized, participatory, and experimentalist styles of partnership between government and business. To push economic vanguardism beyond the social and geographic frontiers of the conventional vanguards, we need national and local governments able to help create the missing conditions and to help form the missing agents.

We should reject the false choice between the idea of arms'-length government (embraced by free-market orthodoxy) and the contrasting practice (exemplified by some of the northeast Asian "tiger economies") of a centralized economic bureaucracy, formulating industrial and trade strategy, subsidizing credit, and rewarding promise or success with favor. Instead, we should develop a broad-based and market-friendly effort to lift up the rearguard.

Such an effort would have four elements. The first element is the focus on child protection and educational renewal, and the use of child-centered support programs to encourage the development of community groups. Without an organized local society, able to take care of its children, vanguardism outside the vanguard has no chance. A second element is the creation of technical support centers, reskilling services, and small-business incubators to assist private initative outside the advanced sectors of the economy. A major responsibility of such centers would be to help identify and propagate successful work and business practices as they emerged. A third element is the organization of associations among firms. The associated businesses would pool financial, commercial, and technical resources in some areas while competing with one another in others. A fourth element is the broadening of access to finance and technology, through the establishment of independently administered venture-capital funds, chartered to invest in the rearguard and to conserve and grow the resources with which they would be endowed. Experience suggests that, with accountable but independent management and properly diversified investment portfolios, such funds can achieve high rates of return on their endowments.

Different kinds of property relations between the funds and their client firms would develop over time. Some funds would keep a distance from their clients, auctioning capital off to a diversified group of entrepreneurs with the best prospects of making good on the investment, and taking equity stakes in the firms they helped start, as any venture capitalist would. Other funds would nurture close and lasting relations with a group of similar small businesses, becoming the financial and technical brain and arm of a little confederation of firms. Property would be divided up in different ways between funds and firms, and different regimes of private and social property and decentralized initiative would begin to coexist experimentally within the economy.

The outcome of such experiments is not the suppression of the market; it is the democratizing and diversification of the market. It is the road to closing the gap between vanguard and rearguard. It is the refusal to let the global reshaping of production continue on an exclusive and divisive course.

AN ORGANIZED SOCIETY AND AN EMPOWERED LABOR FORCE: THE TOOLS AND RESOURCES OF ASSOCIATION

A disorganized society cannot generate conceptions of its alternative futures or act upon them. Organization is power, a power essential to a vigorous democracy. Disorganization is surrender to drift, to accident, to fate. America has always been famous for its wealth of voluntary associations. Today, however, Americans are more disassociated than ever before: living alone, often without friends, and less engaged in unions, clubs, fraternal orders, and even local government or parent-teacher associations. Only in church, synagogue, and mosque attendance do the numbers seem to hold up, faith in God having outlived, for many Americans, hope in society.

It is not enough to call for a rebirth of the spirit of voluntary association, for although we may call the spirit, it may not come. Instead, we need to reexamine and reconstruct the institutional setting in which association thrives. Reforms in labor law, local government law, and federal tax law can help renew the force and democratize the scope of associational activity in America.

Such reforms can also diminish the force of a striking and troubling feature of associational life in all contemporary industrial democracies. The associations with a message for society at large—clubs and churches as well as political parties—remain detached from the everyday world of work and production. Practical associations involved in this everyday world—firms and unions—lack such a message; their job is to make money and defend the interests of their members. If the established rules of contract and corporate law that people use to create and maintain practical associations are indeed like a language, capable of expressing any thought, then the problem is that those who speak this language may have little to say, while those who have something to say are unable to speak it.

Society should be independently organized outside the government: a simple idea with complicated and controversial implications. One major site of organization is work. Labor laws need to be strengthened, not to deepen divisions between a minority of relatively privileged workers in traditional industry and everyone else, but to facilitate unionization everywhere. As temporary work increases in many sectors of the economy, we need to reform the labor laws to encourage the unionization of temporary workers and to ensure the blend of legal regulation of the employment relation and collective bargaining with the employer that is appropriate to their circumstances. More generally, we have to create a structure in which union representation of workers and collaborative profit sharing with workers come to be seen as complementary rather than incompatible approaches. Otherwise, we shall have allowed a contest between cooperation at work and association among workers to develop at the heart of industry, threatening the project of greater economic democracy in America.

An emphasis on early and continuing education and reskilling rather than on job tenure, the development of varied forms of worker protection suited to the circumstances of a segmented labor force, and a commitment to generalize the principle of worker participation in company profits can combine to reverse one of the most antidemocratic trends in recent American life: the decrease of the wage take from national income.

Moreover, this trend can be reversed without threatening the high employment levels the United States has happily achieved. The ability to raise the real value of wages, without threatening jobs and economic growth or risking inflation, will be futher strengthened if we succeed in replacing all payroll taxes by the consumption-oriented taxation we advocate.

What we must resist at any cost is the entrenchment of stark divisions between insiders—relatively privileged, organized workers with jobs in the capital- and knowledge-rich sectors of the economy—and outsiders—workers with unstable, dead-end jobs in the capital- and knowledge-poor sectors. It is a division that has helped bring European social democracy to grief.

Traditional social democrats often fight for something close to job tenure for workers with the good jobs and promote, under the slogan of stakeholding, a mini-constitutionalism of the firm: consumer groups and local communities as well as workers would have a say or even a veto over management decisions. It is a formula that sets up a tension between defending workers' rights and promoting economic flexibility and innovation. Moreover, it is predicated on a division between insiders and outsiders and can help reinforce it. Instead of enshrining job tenure, we want to enhance the capabilities of workers through devices such as government-supported continuous reskilling and social-endowment accounts. Instead of a rigid scheme of checks and balances in corporate governance, we propose radically to decentralize and democratize access to productive resources and opportunities through means such as the public-private venture-capital funds and technical support centers we earlier described.

If work is one site of voluntary association, community life is another. We could, for example, create legal mechanisms for the selection of community councils or neighborhood associations outside the structure of local government. Such councils could be elected on a neighborhood basis to engage individual citizens as well as community groups in the solution of the social—not the physical or financial—problems of the neighborhood: for example, working with the police to set up community policing, identifying children in trouble and referring them or their families to the right sources of public or private assistance, and intervening with hospitals, insurers, and bureaucracies when the old and the sick need help. This work would be neither continuous nor paid. It would be a form of social leadership, somewhere in between private charity and public office. Those who performed it would have, as a matter of law, only advisory power but, as a matter of practical effect, as much influence as their organizing efforts allowed them to exert.

Private philanthropy has been a powerful engine of voluntary action in the United States. It survives, however, on a tax favor. Thus, its consequence is to magnify the voice of the rich, allowing them to ride their social and cultural hobbyhorses. Thanks to the tax laws, their poorer fellow citizens co-sign these gifts whether they want to or not and whether they know it or not. Why not democratize the tax favor? For every tax-deducted dollar that the donor were allowed to use as he wished, a certain portion of the donor's dollars would have to go into a common fund, with the percentage calculated to preserve the force of the tax incentive. That fund, with decentralized governance and independent trustees drawn from every walk of American life, would finance social groups who applied to it for help—through, for example, matching funds or matching commitments of free labor time—to carry out their own charitable activities. The disincentive to private contributions would be limited; the impact upon the resource base of voluntary action in America, immense.

POLITICS, MONEY, AND MEDIA:
QUICKENING THE TEMPO OF DEMOCRACY

For better and worse, Americans revere their Constitution. They early rejected Thomas Jefferson's advice to replace the Constitution completely every few generations. As a result, they hesitate to fiddle with the set-up of the government, and they often prefer to revise (or rather to let Supreme Court justices revise) their Constitution by reinterpreting it rather than by changing it outright.

There are many constitutional reforms that would be worth discussing if the American antipathy to constitutional redesign were less severe. Consider one such example. Admittedly outside the agenda of feasible contemporary concerns, it nevertheless suggests both the price of constitutional conservatism and the possible direction of political reform. Morever, it clarifies the vision underlying the here-and-now political innovations we do propose further ahead.

Madison's scheme for the Constitution combined two principles: an insistence upon the dispersal of political power and a plan to slow politics down, by establishing a rough correspondence between the transformative reach of a political project and the severity of the constitutional obstacles it has to overcome in the course of its execution. Both principles combine in the system of "checks and balances" among branches of government: Franklin Roosevelt, for example, had to wage a tremendous struggle until he got the Supreme Court as well as the Congress on his side, and he had an economic and social disaster working for him.

These two principles—the fragmentation of political power and the slowing down of political change— could, however, be disconnected, in the interests of a deepened democracy. We might want to keep the first principle and rid ourselves of the second. For example, think of the following way to combine characteristics of the presidential and parliamentary systems of government. If the president and the Congress disagree about a program of reform for the country, either of the two elected branches of government can call early elections, but then both branches have to run. The idea is to resolve the impasse quickly, through the prompt engagement of the electorate in its resolution, rather than to perpetuate it in divided government until the next regular election.

To follow the logic of the remedy, we might make voting mandatory, as it is in many contemporary democracies, with the penalty of a fine for the violation of the duty. Failure to vote would, therefore, be sanctioned less severely than, for example, refusal to do jury duty. The obligation to come to the polling station, however, is intended to achieve a good that is at least as great as serving on juries: to prevent the government from being elected by a minority, given that over half the adult citizenry now fails to vote in the United States. That a citizen should have to turn his mind for a few moments, every now and then, to the affairs of the Republic—with the privilege of abstaining in the voting booth—seems a tiny measure of intrusion to accept in exchange for a huge advance in civic engagement. Comparative experience suggests that, once the law directs people to vote, they get into the habit. In no democracy that has adopted such a rule has there ever been a majority in favor of its revocation.

The combined effect of these changes would be to quicken the tempo and raise the energy level of American democracy, while maintaining or even strengthening the fundamental mechanism for making governmental power decentralized and accountable. It will not happen, at least not anytime soon, but it points in a direction. We offer four connected proposals to move American democracy in this direction.

First, establish public financing of political campaigns. Public financing is more effective than the attempt to tighten the policing of private money, especially when combined with our next suggestion, extended free access to television time. It is a minor expense, with vast equalizing and limit-breaking potential for American politics. The best criterion for the distribution of such public funding is a standard intermediate between the present representation of the political parties at the level of goverment—federal, state, or local—at which they are running and a standard of arithmetical equality—the same for all.

Second, give the political parties and their candidates ample free time on television. Fight in the legislatures and the courts to get this time freely given by the networks and channels, as a condition of their license rather than as a service to be paid by the taxpayers. Americans need a public space in which to discuss their shared problems, and television has become the space that matters most. In Brazil, for example, fifty minutes a day of television and radio on all channels are blocked out for the parties and candidates forty-five days before an election. The primitive technology and the indifferent content of many of the political talks have not prevented the campaign programs from maintaining a substantial audience. The voters learn, and so do the politicians. The perversity of the sound bite is reversed when candidates for major national office are required to spend many hours on the air; in the surprisingly intimate medium of television, it is hard to disguise yourself for long.

Third, lower the legal, constitutional, and ideological barriers to experimental, localized, and temporary reversals and combinations of governmental and private responsibilities. If, for example, municipal sanitation services can be contracted out to private business, research and development can also be conducted by joint ventures of governmental agencies, nonprofit organizations such as universities, and private businesses. Venture capital—investment in start-up firms—can be arranged by decentralized funds and support centers, with independent management, a mixed public-private character, and special responsibility for the development of the economic rearguard.

Many such reversals and combinations of function should be tried out locally and temporarily. Different trial solutions to the same problems should be allowed to coexist. How else can we find out what works? Much more is at stake here than efficiency of public administration. The point is to tap the repressed potential for decentralized partnership among individuals, government, and business, rejecting the model of arms'-length regulation as the only acceptable way in which government can relate to society. One project will lead to another. Small successes will give impulse to larger ambitions. American federalism—far from being a pretext to stop social experiments in the name of "states' rights"—will turn out to be a special case of the larger idea of "many laboratories."

Fourth, change the attitudes and the practices about party politics so that the political parties—the two big parties as well as emerging third parties—can become the authors and agents of real alternatives. We need not choose between the political party as the disciplined instrument of a purist ideology and the political party as a syndicate of professional office-seekers catering to an amorphous assortment of special interests. Americans are unlikely ever to adopt proportional representation—the electoral system that distributes legislative seats in proportion to votes for parties. They are even less likely to embrace the closed-list version of such systems—where the voter votes only for a party and the parties determine the priority of the candidates on its slate. However, the present scheme of election primaries in the United States makes sense only if Americans have given up on political parties and the coherent options that it would be the task of the parties to forge and implement. Adopted in the name of grassroots democracy, this scheme robs the parties of any prospect of strong internal organization and programmatic definition.

Who knows the name of the chairman of either major political party in the United States? He or she is invariably a creature of the president in office or a caretaker until the next presidential candidate shows up, and, in either event, a hapless hustler for money. Members of Congress are routinely reelected, although the electorate professes disgust with the political class, because the public expects from them little more than service to local interests and conformity to certain minimum ideological tests in their voting behavior. The result is that, although Americans are able to discuss, for example, an isolated issue like whether to allow physicians to help the terminally ill commit suicide, they lack the political instruments with which to define, collectively, different roads for their country to take. Should such a demarcation of national possibilities be just the work of a clever politician, sensing a change in national mood and grasping at the latest fashions from the universities? Or should it result from a more inclusive and sustained conversation in the country?

The political parties should assert greater authority

over slates, candidates, candidate selection, and party platforms. At the same time, however, they should open themselves up to internal democracy, organizing national elections among their members to choose their leaders and directions. The shift from an emphasis upon candidate-by-candidate choice through primaries to an emphasis upon party democracy and party leadership would trigger the organization of movements and factions within each party to contest such party elections. The defeated groups would clamor for minority representation in the party councils or establish third parties. The temperature of American politics would rise, and its repertory of programmatic alternatives broaden.

In this great country every privilege is suspect, and ordinary men and women are known to be not so ordinary after all. Tinkering is both a habit and a creed, and experimentalism joins hands with democracy. An America triumphant in the world nevertheless seems unable to solve its own problems. Class injustice, racial hatred, and rationalized selfishness thrive today in a climate of disillusionment and feed on an experience of disengagement and disconnection. In this circumstance, the work of the progressives is to speak, within and outside the Democratic party, for a clear alternative.

Not for some impossible, romantic dream of a different "system." Not for the last-ditch defense of every part of the New Deal compromise in American politics. Not for the Republican agenda—or the doctrine of the one true way—with a human face. Not for the humanization of the inevitable. But for a practical view of how, step by step, and piece by piece, to democratize the American economy and reenergize American democracy.

To understand your country you must love it. To love it you must, in a sense, accept it. To accept it as it is, however, is to betray it. To accept your country without betraying it, you must love it for that in it which shows what it might become. America—this monument to the genius of ordinary men and women, this place where hope becomes capacity, this long halting, turn of the no into the yes—needs citizens who love it enough to reimagine and remake it.